# RMS Techn

C000143619

## A Quick Guide To
## Understanding
# IT Security Basics

—— For IT Professionals ——

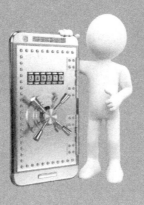

# A Quick Guide To Understanding IT Security Basics For IT Professionals

# Table of Contents

# Introduction

We all need IT security primarily because of our reliance on technology. The average person depends on his gadgets so much that his entire life is in there – his banking passwords, his family, his face, his doctor, the route he takes to get to work and to get home, industry secrets, and so many other kinds of information.

So what would you think would happen if suddenly, someone grabs hold of this information and uses the data for their own good?

The outcome could be disastrous. If a business revolves around sensitive data, the outcome is even more devastating. The good news is that IT security can prevent that kind of disaster.

IT security is defined as the method of implementing measures and systems specially designed to protect information, making sure it doesn't get into the wrong hands. It prevents unauthorized access, inspection, use, modification, disclosure, recording, and/or destruction of data.

In this book, you'll learn about the goals of IT security, as well as the concepts surrounding it.

You'll also have an idea of what the common threats are, where they come from, and how you can stay away from them.

Ways to mitigate threats are also included, especially in this digital age where a wrong click can immediately lead to your data being completely wiped off in just a second.

It also helps to be familiar with the tools and terminologies, and so, you'll find out more about them here.

I'm glad that you're taking steps to be familiar with IT security. Soon, you'll learn how to protect yourself from all the people out there with malicious intent. Let's all protect our data so that no one can steal our information ever again.

It's definitely better to be prepared, don't you think?

Thanks for downloading this book. I hope you enjoy it!

# Chapter 1 – What is IT Security?

Look around you. What do you see? Almost everything is connected to the Internet and the technologies related to it. People young and old have their own mobile devices. You'd find computers almost everywhere. Bits of information are stored on databases, accessible over the Internet.

It's vital that sensitive information is kept out of the wrong hands. Hackers today are becoming more and more cunning as the days pass. Proper IT security and privacy measures, when implemented, will greatly help in preventing data leakage.

Let's understand things better by understanding what information security (IT) is, and what factors are involved in it.

# What is IT Security?

IT Security is a group of cybersecurity strategies that help prevent unauthorized access to organizational assets, such as networks, and stops sophisticated hackers from gaining access to the system.

IT security and information security sound similar and are related to one another even though each of them has a specific scope to deal with. The former is more of securing one's digital data through computer network security , while the latter refers to both tools and processes designed to protect sensitive personal and business information from invasion.

IT and data security can cover several points, including but not limited to the following:

- One's genetic material
- Information about one's residence and personal location
- Healthcare records
- Criminal justice records
- Financial information, transactions, and data
- Personal communications
- Browsing history
- Location-based services data

IT security comes in different types:

- Network Security - This is used to prevent both malicious and unauthorized users from gaining access to your network. This type ensures that reliability, integrity, and usability are not compromised and harmed in any way. Through this, hackers won't access data inside your network, and won't be able to view or change anything.
- Cloud Security - Today, information is not just stored inside physical devices; most of them are stored in the cloud as well – this means users are connected directly to the Internet, and that they aren't covered by the usual security stack. Through cloud security, SaaS (software-as-a-service) applications, as well as the public cloud, are better secured.
- Endpoint Security - This kind of security gives protection at the device level. Devices that can be covered by this include mobile phones, tablets, desktop computers, and laptops. This stops your devices from accessing malicious networks that are possible threats to you and your organization. Examples of this include device management software and advanced malware protection.

- Application Security – With application security, applications are coded only at the time of creation to make them secure as possible and to ensure their safety from attacks. The security layer involves an app's code evaluation, as well as identifies the possible vulnerabilities that could exist within the software.

Each type has its own contribution in making data more secure for every user. Each has its own department and level, and without one, the other areas may need support and reinforcement to work perfectly.

## IT Security Frameworks

It can be quite overwhelming to build and run IT security programs, especially since they come with various tasks and responsibilities.

To effectively create and maintain these programs, there should be a hybrid security framework that helps achieve business objectives, as well as define policies and procedures designed for the controls inside the organization. This framework should outline particular security controls as well as regulatory requirements that have an impact on the business.

Here are some of the common security frameworks, as well as how they are constructed:

## Control Objectives for Information and Related Technology (COBIT)

Produced in 1996, COBIT is a high-level framework created with the intent of finding and mitigating risks. COBIT was developed initially for IT governance professionals to lessen technical risks, but eventually, it evolved to a standard that aligns IT with business goals.

Its latest revision was made to address best practices in relation to align IT processes and functions and have them linked to business strategies.

Compared to other security frameworks, COBIT is not as widely followed; it often is used by the finance industry in compliance with Sarbanes-Oxley and other related standards. It lacks enough informative practical advice, but if your business is after a formal framework for risk management, then this'll work for you.

## National Institute of Standards and Technology (NIST)

The NIST, first published in 1990, helps federal government agencies in the US to comply with FIPS or Federal Information Processing Standards. Viewed as mature and comprehensive, the NIST has evolved for two decades and is even considered the "father" of other security frameworks.

The security standards and guidelines for this framework could have been specially established for federal information systems and government agencies, but it's also followed widely in the private sector. It's believed to generally represent the best practices in the industry.

International Standards Organization (ISO)

The ISO framework is one of the most popular security standards. It's a set of broad standards that cover best practices in confidentiality, privacy, and IT security published together with the International Electrotechnical Commission.

The ISO intends to help organizations address the risks using the appropriate controls.

## IT Security Governing Bodies

When it comes to IT security, discussing its governance can be quite vague as there's not one specific group that oversees it all. Each organization, even the government, has its own IT department that controls how data is protected as well as how laws are being created in relation to it.

To understand which law or organization handles the concern, you should first assess what the concern is, as well as check the boundaries in place. Not every law covers a concern, usually there's a specific law that pertains to every issue. Here are some of the regulations that deal with IT security, as well as its scope:

## Sarbanes Oxley Act (SOX)

*What it is* : The Sarbanes Oxley Act is a set of requirements that cover the rules and responsibilities of the directors, state penalties should there be misconduct, and give instructions to the Securities and Exchange Commission regarding regulations on how public corporations should adhere to the law. It specifically requires companies to maintain their financial records for seven years.

*Scope* : It affects public accounting firms, US public company boards and management.

## Health Insurance Portability and Accountability Act (HIPAA)

*What it is* : You'd think this doesn't have to do anything with IT security since it deals with healthcare, but it actually intends to simplify the process as more and more organizations are making the switch to electronic data. To add, it also protects the patients' privacy as it also secures their information.

*Scope* : This covers any company or organization that has to do anything with healthcare data, i.e., insurance companies, doctors' offices, employers, and business associates.

## Family Educational Rights and Privacy Act (FERPA)

*What it is* : This is a federal law that protects the student education records' privacy. This gives the parents' protection regarding their children's education records, e.g., transcripts, report cards, class schedules, disciplinary records, and family and contact information.

*Scope* : This covers institutions, mostly postsecondary, including academies, universities, technical schools, vocational schools, and seminaries.

Payment Card Industry Data Security Standard (PCI-DSS)

*What it is* : The PCI-DSS is a group of 12 regulations that aim to reduce fraud as well as protect clients' credit card information. This makes vendors aware, understand, and implement standards that protect everyone from theft and data breaches.

*Scope* : It covers companies that handle obtain personal and financial information in relation to credit cards, such as point-of-sale vendors, hardware and software developers, merchants of various sizes, and other financial institutions that handle processing payments.

Gramm Leach Bliley Act (GLBA)

*What it is* : The GLBA allows investment banks, commercial banks, and insurance companies to be under the same company. It mandates that these companies ensure the safety and security of their customers' private information.

*Scope* : This covers "financial institutions", i.e., companies offering financial products or services such as insurance, financial or investment advice and assistance, and/or loans.

General Data Protection Regulation (GDPR)

*What it is* : The GDPR is a massive law implemented in 2016 by the European Union, stating rules and regulations on how companies should manage and share clients' personal data.

*Scope* : In theory, it only covers EU citizens' data, but because of the Internet's global nature, this means almost every online service is affected, and these companies have to adapt.

The laws governing IT security are just not limited to these; these are just some of the laws and regulations that govern IT security, particularly data handling and privacy. These policies make sure that acquiring, handling, and storage of data is not abused and properly implemented.

# Chapter 2 – Why We Need IT Security

From an industrial economy, we have shifted to the digital world. Today, you no longer need to keep numerous notebooks to store your data. You don't have to write down things to keep track of them.

SO long as you have your digital devices on hand, then you can already feel at ease knowing you have everything on your fingertips. This dependence on technology is just one of the reasons why there's the need to value IT security. In this chapter, you'll learn why IT security is of utmost importance, especially today when everything seems to be bound by technology.

**New threats, which were once considered unrealistic and unreasonable, have now become possible.**

Years ago, security threats that were considered unrealistic and unreasonable were only laughed at.

A single virus after computers all over the world? *Impossible* . A single hacker able to control computers at different locations? *You must be out of your mind* .

Years ago, you'd only consider them as plots for science fiction movies. Now, they could happen anytime. Artificial intelligence is no longer limited to works of fiction; it's now a technology that advanced hackers can utilize and take advantage of.

**People have become reliant on their security to technology.**

The reliance of people to technology has become greater nowadays. Let's take smart phones, for example. Today, people rarely write down mobile numbers – they save the numbers on their phones. Office records and other pertinent information are also saved online, with other relevant data.

What would happen if suddenly, someone gains access to their mobile phones and personal computers? What if someone suddenly has the power to check every detail of a particular individual?

We are solely responsible for protecting our information. We are in charge of our personal computers, phones and other gadgets; we know how we could protect them. But what if we're already dealing with the global diffusion of data? What about those details stored in the cloud?

This greater need to rely on technology would also come with the greater need to protect data. We should understand what should be protected, how it should be protected, and who has the responsibility of protecting it.

**You wouldn't want to lose money because of security threats and vulne rabilities .**

Your company will be financially sound if your infrastructure can start running efficiently with the least amount of downtime possible. Look at it this way – if your employees can't work due to network issues, then your business w ill lose money. If you lose valuable information, your clients could lose faith in you. There are also cases such as the Bangladesh Bank Heist in which literally millions of dollars were lost due to a security breach.

How unfortunate would it be for you and your company if everything crashes just because malware has infected your system? What more if it involved personal data and breached laws, one of which being GDPR? You'll not only spend money on fines and penalties, but also to recreate your system and bring it back to how it was. Plus, what if you ended up losing clients because they decided they can no longer rely on a breached company?

The possibilities are definitely endless. The good news though is that you can still prevent those things from happening through the installation of reliable products. Security threats will always be there and so in these cases, prevention will always be better than cure.

**More attacks are bound to happen.**

For the past few years, we've already witnessed several attempts of these attacks penetrating security systems.

Where do these hackers get the courage to continue this behavior? They feed on new startups and businesses that think their security is good enough, especially when their priority is to establish and strengthen their business first.

What's wrong with that set-up, then?

If your focus is on strengthening your business with digital factors incorporated in them, yet you don't prioritize IT security, then you'll end up losing rather than winning. You don't take care of security updates, while hackers on the other hand stay updated, and become even more dangerous as the days pass.

Cyber criminals love to prey on small businesses, and more so if these small businesses are hired by big firms for their services – hackers use this partnership to bypass the big firms' security systems.

The more the smaller companies neglect their security systems, the more attacks are bound to happen, hence, the need for a stronger IT security system to stop hackers from further taking action.

Because we have reached the digital age, attacks on the cyber world will continue to occur. And so, everyone must learn how to be vigilant and understand the threats as much as possible so we can shield ourselves from the problems they would bring.

# Chapter 3 – The Goals of IT Security

This chapter will discuss the goals of IT security. These goals are the security mechanisms that will help you deal with the possibility of attacks occurring, or when you get to face the attacks themselves.

IT security has three goals: prevention, detection, and recovery.

**First Goal: Prevention**

Having prevention measures in place means the attack will likely fail.

Here's to illustrate this further: let's say a hacker attempts to break into your system through the Internet. Your system, however, is not connected to the Internet. And so, the attack has been stopped.

In preventing security threats and attacks, there are mechanisms in place that only those authorized has to perform correctly and precisely; unauthorized users can't override or change it in any way. Because attackers can't defeat the mechanism, they can't change the data that the mechanism protects.

Preventive measures, however, can be cumbersome and time-consuming. For example, instead of just switching your computer on and going straight to whatever tasks you're supposed to do, you'd still have to enter a password for verification. What if you forgot the password? You'd be locked out and you can't access your data.

Still, it's better to get locked out and just have it reset after proving your identity rather than have someone get into your files and modify them, don't you think?

**Second Goal: Detection**

Detection does two things: one, it lets you know if there's an attack that you can't prevent, and two, it gives you an idea on how effective your preventive measures are.

Setting detection mechanisms means that you are aware and that you've accepted that attacks CAN and WILL occur. What you want is to know if there is an existing attack so it can be reported, and you can do something about it.

Detection mechanisms will let you know about the attack's nature, severity, and possible effects on your system. It monitors your systems and checks if there are any signs of attempts of attacks.

Let's take the earlier example to illustrate this further. You are asked to enter the password as a security measure. You fail to enter the password three times. On your third attempt, you receive a warning. At that moment, the system is also alerted that someone is trying to login without passing verification procedures.

The drawback of detection mechanisms, however, is that they don't prevent the system from being compromised – it only monitors data and leaves it up to you to perform the necessary action.

## Third Goal: Recovery

There are two forms of recovery.

The first form deals with stopping attacks, as well as assessing or repairing damages caused by the attack. Let's say a hacker deletes a file. The recovery response is to restore the deleted file using backup documents.

This makes recovery a complex procedure – the nature of attacks differ, and so, the types and extent of the damage could be difficult to identify. Plus, the attacker can come back, so as a part of recovery, you'd still have to identify and fix the vulnerabilities that the attacker used to penetrate the system.

During these times, the system would possibly not function well. It may scan itself to see the damage that had taken place, as well as possible recovery methods that can be implemented.

On the other hand, the second form of recovery is harder to implement because of the computer systems' complexities. In this form, the systems would still proceed to function normally, but it may choose to disable non-essential processes when necessary.

These three goals of IT security – prevention, detection, and recovery – all work together to ensure IT security processes are in effect and are functioning well.

# Chapter 4 – General IT Security Concepts

When dealing with IT security, you'll often encounter the "CIA Triad": **C**onfidentiality, **I**ntegrity, and **A**vailability.

## CONFIDENTIALITY

When we speak of confidentiality of information, we're talking about protecting data from being disclosed to unauthorized parties.

In today's world, information has a bigger value. Everyone has secrets they'd prefer to stay hidden, or at least not want everyone to know – we're talking about personal information i.e., physical address, date of birth and social security numbers, bank account details, credit card numbers, and other government documents.

Your goal is to ensure the protection of these important documents, and that is within the scope of *confidentiality* .

Confidentiality is the first goal of IT security. It works by protecting the data of businesses, either in motion or in storage, from unauthorized people. The confidentiality goal ensures that data will only be accessible to the people who are authorized to use it, and only to those intended to receive it.

Basically, confidentiality allows access to data only to those who have permission and credentials to do so. It's the ability to hide information from those who don't have the authority to view it.

Confidentiality may be the most obvious goal of IT security, knowing how essential personal information is to everyone, but it definitely is the most attacked – perhaps because of the same reason. Hackers understand how powerful it must be to gain everyone's personal details, hence the need to penetrate the systems and use the data for their own good.

Confidentiality has three key concepts: authorization, authentication, and encryption.

- Authentication: The authentication process helps prove the identity of a user. Through authentication, you'll prove that a user is indeed who they claim to be. This process makes certain that each authorized user has their own user IDs and passwords, and could also implement biometrics to ensure proper security. Almost every website requires authentication. If someone didn't pass authentication, then they'd only be allowed to view and access public information.

- Authorization: This is the process that establishes access controls to make sure that user actions will only be performed by the people within their roles. You may have been authenticated, but that doesn't mean you can perform every action or see every piece of data. You're only able to access and modify only those things that you've been given authorization for.

- Encryption: This is the method that ensures confidentiality. This stops snooping eyes from viewing the actual data, regardless if it's at rest or in transit. This protects the confidentiality of the data. Banks, for example, make sure to use the HTTPS connection so every data sent back and forth by the client and the bank are all encrypted. Sensitive details such as account numbers, Social Security numbers, and other credentials are not readable even to someone who's just eavesdropping on the conversation.

Confidentiality is related to information technology security because the latter requires utmost control on the access to protected information. Every information handed over is precious, and so, it shouldn't be given carelessly to unauthorized individuals.

## **INTEGRITY**

Integrity refers to the trustworthiness of resources or data; it keeps data pure and trustworthy; this protects the system data from being changed intentionally or accidentally. You want to make sure the data stored is both accurate and consistent, and every change authorized and monitored.

Careless changes could lead to unauthorized access and use, plus, errors could arise inside the information database that would possibly affect everything stored.

Examples of integrity checks include balancing batch transactions to ensure all information is not only complete, but also accurately accounted for.

Integrity is related to information technology security because having both accuracy and consistency in the information is because of proper data protection.

Integrity mechanisms are divided into two classes, namely *prevention* and *detection*.

1. Prevention – These mechanisms aim to maintain data integrity by stopping acts, and even attempts, of changing the data without proper authorization.

2. Detection – These mechanisms don't prevent integrity violations; what they do is to inform you when your stored data is no longer trustworthy. They check system events to determine any problems, or they can even check the data itself to see if there are issues within it. They'd either tell you what happened, or would just tell you that the data is now corrupted and/or unusable.

Note that *prevention* takes place when a user attempts to change data when the user has no authorization to change it in the first place. On the other hand, *detection* takes place when an authorized user attempts to make an unauthorized change.

The approach, when it comes to integrity, would be different from that of confidentiality. When it comes to confidentiality, you'd deal with data that could have been compromised. Integrity deals with data accuracy and credibility. It confirms where the data came from, how well it was protected on its source, and how well it's being protected now.

## AVAILABILITY

Availability is all about keeping the data and resources easily accessible, especially during emergencies or disasters. It makes sure that systems work perfectly, and the service won't be denied to those authorized to use it.

When it comes to an operational standpoint, availability pertains to guaranteed bandwidth and/or adequate response time. On a security standpoint, on the other hand, it refers to the ability to protect the systems and recover from an impacting event.

Availability is a major factor for computer operations, and in some cases, can even be an instrument to save lives. Companies should always have contingency plans on hand to ensure they won't ever lose the system's availability.

Contingency Planning

Contingency plans must be put in place to ensure systems are always available. Plans often set involve those in preparation for acts of God such as earthquakes, or accidental events like gas leaks or other related events.

When it comes to availability, IT security professionals deal with these challenges:

- Failures of the equipment during normal use
- Losing information system capabilities due to natural disasters, i.e. , floods, storms, fires, or earthquakes, or human actions such as strikes or bombs
- Denial of Service (DoS) that could have taken place because of intentional attacks or undiscovered implementation flaws (e.g., a programmer writing a program but unaware of a flaw that could lead to program crashes upon entering a specific input command

Having availability guarantees reliable and constant access to information. By making sure that both hardware and software are properly maintained, you'll ensure availability on your systems.

For worst-case scenarios, always have a quick and adaptive recovery plan in place. Of course, this will be most effective when you have a complete recovery plan prepared for your systems should there be problems with availability.

Confidentiality, Integrity, and Availability, or what we know now as the CIA triad, is an essential concept in security. All factors of the CIA triad must be protected in order to have a secure system. Feel free to come up with alternative models that are quite similar to this, as long as the idea of protecting your data is covered.

# Chapter 5 – Common Types of Security Threats

Security threats come in different kinds and forms. They are defined differently, but generally, security threats are malicious events or actions targeted at disrupting the integrity of either personal or corporate security threats. It intends to compromise data for exploitation purposes.

Threats can be present even without the violation taking place. The fact that there's a possibility for the violations to occur means that there should be something in place to guard and protect them.

The kinds of data can vary; examples include contact lists, passwords, or credit card information. Other types include those that could interest advertisers such as your Internet browsing habits.

In this chapter, let's get you familiarized with the different types of security threats.

## Phishing

Phishing attacks come in different forms: sometimes, they appear as a fake website designed similarly to the real website, and sometimes, they come in the form of email messages that make you believe they're from legitimate sources.

What phishing attacks do is to lure you into providing your personal information that's beneficial to them. They'd pretend to be your email service provider or your bank and ask you to click on the links they provided so you can give them your personal data, account information, and even your credit card details.

There's also another form called *spear phishing* . In this form, the criminal would pose as a customer or colleague to convince the victim to visit a website, and then, malicious software will then be downloaded to the victim's computer. The attacker could also pose as an executive, and ask the victim to send confidential information or wire payments .

To lessen your chances of being victimized by phishing attacks, you can go for these techniques:

- Hover over the links but not click them . Place your mouse over the cursor but don't click the link. Hovering over the link will usually show where it would lead you. Does the link look credible? Does it appear trustworthy? Use your judgment in deciphering the URL.
- Analyze the headers. The link appears legit, so you clicked it. Now, you check the email headers, particularly the "Reply to" and the "Return path" parameters. The headers tell you how that email got to your address. Do they lead to the same domain stated in the email?
- Perform 'sandboxing' . If you can, you should perform sandboxing. Just like a child's sandbox, a sandbox environment provides you with a simulated area to test your activities. In this case, you'd be testing the email content. While sandboxing, you can log the activity as you open attachments and click the links on the email.
- Exercise critical thinking. Don't click emails when you are tired, bus y, or too stressed to even think. Always, always analyze every email you're opening. It may look like the real thing, but it's not always the real deal.

If there's one thing that you need to remember about phishing attacks, it's that they will only win if you let them. Don't be fooled.

## Trojan

When someone speaks of a "Trojan horse", they could be pertaining to tricking an individual to bringing them in a securely protected area. When talking about software, the Trojan refers to an attacking code that tricks people into running it through the guise of a legitimate program.

*What It Is:*

The Trojan Horse, or the Trojan, is a form of malware that makes itself appear as legitimate software. They can be employed by hackers and cyber-thieves that try to access your systems.

The Trojan virus is one of the most complex threats you could ever face. If you've heard of SpyEye and Zeus, then those are from the Trojan family. Trojan attacks invade your system by disguising as a legitimate app, but in reality is malicious                              software.

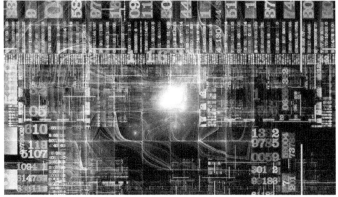

*Image from Kaspersky.com*

Once the Trojan software invades your computer, it can choose to log your keystrokes to save your passwords or even hijack your webcam to record your movements. It can hide from your antivirus program and can stay undetected, as well as in false advertisements.

*The Infection Effects*

How would your systems be infected by a Trojan Horse? Well, as previously mentioned, this is a form of malware that hides behind legitimate software. To gain access to other systems, hackers can use the Trojan horse.

Users are often tricked by a kind of social engineering into having the Trojan installed or executed on their computers. Upon activation, the infection can allow hackers to steal your data, spy on you, and even gain backdoor access to your systems.

Once the Trojan horse has entirely affected your system, your data can either be blocked, modified, copied, or even deleted. Your computers and networks' performance can be disrupted.

*How to Protect Yourself From This Attack*

Protect your systems from a Trojan horse attack by installing anti-malware software. This will then defend your devices, whether they're PCs, Macs, laptops, smartphones, and tablets.

## Ransomware

Another well-known type of security threat is ransomware.

What ransomware does is to lock your files, keep you from gaining access to them, and "kidnaps" them so that you'll have to pay a ransom to get them back, hence the name. You'll see a message stating how the FBI, police, or other official institution has your files, and that you'll have to pay them a fine to get the files back and to prevent persecution.

Ransomware often hides inside emails with malicious attachments, but they're also found inside website pop-ups. You'd know if you've become a victim – the message will be quite obvious. The message will be plastered on your screen, and you won't be able to go to your files.

Image from bleepingcomputer.com

## There's Ransomware in Your Files! What Do You Do?

What if you've been trapped by ransomware? What should you do?

*First, don't pay the ransom.* You could be in a hurry to gain access to your files, but settling the ransom won't help. You could, but in the end, the files will still stay encrypted even if you do.

*Second, get in touch with experts.* The usual antivirus tools usually won't help. You can try, but they often don't work. It's better to reach out to an IT engineer to have it fixed. They can try to remove the ransomware, recover your data, and repair the machine.

Just to set your expectations, the ransomware can be removed, but not all times you can recover your files. That's why you should always have a backup of your files so you'll have a recovery plan in case this happens.

*How to Protect Your Files from Ransomware*

Here are some ways on how you can protect your files from ransomware:

- Don't provide your personal details when answering unsolicited phone calls, text messages, instant messages, or emails. Malicious hackers will attempt to trick you and your employees into installing malware, or even claim that they're from IT to gain intelligence from attacks.
- Your servers should have content filtering and scanning. If there are incoming emails, they should be scanned for threats and attachments that appear threatening should be blocked.
- All software and systems should be kept up-to-date through relevant patches. Regular patches of vulnerable software are essential to prevent infection.

Small and medium businesses are often targets of ransomware

## Virus

These days, if a computer is infected, the average person automatically says it was a virus that had penetrated their systems. The word "virus" has become an umbrella term, but it's actually one form of security threat among many.

Viruses are usually programs sent through either a downloaded file or an email attachment. Your computer can be infected by viruses simply by visiting a malicious website. The name "virus" comes from its capability of infecting rapidly – it can spread through networks, email, as well as through connected computers.

Viruses send spam emails, corrupt and even steal data from your computer , disable your security settings, or even delete all the contents of your hard drive. They can scan and seek your personal information e.g., passwords, and hijack your web browser.

To be protected from viruses, a reliable antivirus program should be installed. Because the virus threats are constantly changing, there will always be risks and so, you should always be updated.

Here are the signs that might indicate your computer was being infected by viruses:

- your computer takes a long time to boot,
- it restarts all on its own, or
- the computer doesn't even boot at all.
- files, data, and programs are disappearing,
- constant crashes, or

- the home browser of your computer suddenly gets changed.

Make sure to always have an updated virus protection program. Run a scan periodically to keep everything in tiptop shape. If your virus scan ends up finding nothing yet signs point to a virus, then it's better to seek the help of an IT engineer.

## Spam

It's not the canned meat you love (or perhaps hate). This threat is so special that there's a special email folder for it. Yes, we're talking about spam.

*What is Spam?*

The term 'spam' is used to refer to unsolicited and unwanted communication sent using an online medium.

It's a form of intrusive advertising in which spammers harvest the recipient addresses from sources that are publicly accessible, use programs that are able to collect addresses, or even use dictionaries to make automated guesses for domains.

The harmless ones are those sent to you just to promote products and services, usually received because they were given your personal details, which of course, included your email.

The one you should steer clear from are those emails that attempt to gather your personal information and gain access to your systems. Spam emails often forge or even conceal the origin of their mails to circumvent laws, anti-spammer lists, or service provider regulations.

## How Spam Becomes a Security Threat

Unlike those spam emails that only intend to flood your mail with promotions, sales, and the like, harmful spam emails come from computers infected by viruses.

Spammers and virus makers sometimes join forces to make the lives of innocent computer users suffer – the latter would then be "zombies" that send spam, hence spreading the infection. Spam also ends up blocking communication channels, creating traffic that has to be paid by either the user or the provider.

Spam undoubtedly fills your inbox with useless and senseless emails, but other than that, it can modify or even steal your information by obtaining details on your Contact lists and even change the results on your search engine pages.

## Case in Point: Runbox

Aside from taking up space in your mailboxes and giving you headaches through those unwanted emails, spam can also have other indirect yet lingering effects on both email users and services.

Let's take *Runbox* as an example. Like most email service providers, Runbox fell victim to forgery. Spammers used special software to come up with false email headers as well as From addresses. They confused email servers, domain administrators, and spam victims through false server names and domains.

It's also common to hear of email accounts or addresses to be hijacked. Affected addresses usually claim to be related to Runbox even when they're not, and Runbox is first to state that they don't distribute clients' email addresses and don't give out spam directly or indirectly.

Falsified messages also victimize email users, claiming to come from service administrators that state how the user's account is closed and that the user has to do a specific action to have it reopened. Messages like these shouldn't be opened, and must be ignored or better yet, deleted.

## *How to Fight Spam*

So how do you prevent spam? One way is to always verify both sender and recipient information of suspicious messages. Spam messages are often sent using falsified email accounts to hide the actual sender, plus with several hidden recipients in the BCC field of the email.

Another spam prevention method is to use trustworthy firewalls and antivirus programs. They will protect you not just from spam emails but also from other major security threats.

Have you received emails you didn't ask for? Don't respond to them. You probably have an idea of your subscriptions, newsletters, or other correspondence. If you receive anything that you're not expecting , then delete it immediately. This is most especially when you receive emails with subjects "Need funds", or "Need assistance". Don't mention your emails in chats or newsletters. If you need to send an email to a group of people, then use the BCC field to hide the names from other recipients. Your personal information should never be given out to unreliable sources.

## Spyware

Spyware is a form of unwanted software that penetrates your computing device. This also steals both your Internet usage data and your sensitive information. Spyware is a form of malware – it gathers your personal data and relays them to data firms, advertisers, or external users.

There are different reasons why hackers go for spyware. Spyware is often used to track and even sell your Internet usage data, capture your financial information, and steal your personal identity by monitoring your Internet activity, tracking both your login and password information, and spying on you, as well as your sensitive data.

Spyware hacks lead to identity theft or credit card fraud. If you've been a victim of those, don't despair – you're not alone. According to cybercrime statistics, in 20 countries, around 970 million people have been affected by cybercrime, losing around $172 billion in the process.

*How do you get spyware?*

Most devices can be affected by spyware, whether they're PCs, Mac computers, or Android or iOS devices. It may be true that the Windows operating system is the one that's more susceptible to attacks, but hackers have been finding ways to infiltrate the iOS system as well.

There are several ways on how you could be infected by spyware:

- Drive-by Download – Through this manner, a pop-up window or a site will appear that attempts to download and set up the spyware in the machine. If your computer has the proper security, you'd get a message from your browser informing you of the attempts, asking you if you can go ahead and sell it. An unprotected computer would just go ahead and install the spyware.

- Browser Add-ons – Your Web browser often offers enhancements, such as additional search boxes, animated content, or toolbars. There are times when they indeed deliver and do what they're supposed to do, but some come with spyware elements. The nasty ones are known as 'browser hijackers' as they take over your system and are difficult to remove.

- Software Piggybacks – There are applications that install spyware as a part of the usual installation procedure. If you're not too careful, you'll see that you're installing something else other than the software you originally wanted. This often happens with free software that serves as an alternative to paid ones.

- Pretends to be Anti-Spyware – This often hits computer users hard when software pretends to be something that terminates spyware turn out to be spyware. You'd think you're all protected, when in fact you're more vulnerable than ever. Upon running the tool, you'll be informed your computer is clean but spyware is installed on its own.

Be careful when installing or downloading files to make sure that you won't be putting yoursel f at risk. Not all software that claims to do something will actually live up to its word.

*What Spyware Does*

At a minimum, spyware runs an application as soon as you boot your computer, hogging processor power and RAM. You'll also deal with endless pop-up ads, making your browser lag and become slow, to the point that you'll almost give up using it. It'll be invisible – you won't know that it's there.

Spyware can target financial institutions and seek information from infected computers. They can capture computer activity such as the websites visited, search history, chatroom exchanges, email discussions, system credentials, and keystrokes. They capture screenshots at scheduled intervals. Image, audio, and video transmission can also be possible.

**Snooping**

Snooping is another common security threat. Also referred to as "sniffing", snooping is having unauthorized access to the data of another individual or company. It's somehow similar to *eavesdropping* , but snooping isn't just about having access to data as it is being transmitted.

Snooping can be as simple as looking at the screen of someone's who's sending an email, or as complicated as using software to monitor the activity of a computer or a network.

Some cases of snooping are 'legitimate'. Some companies snoop on their employees to monitor the usage of company PCs and track Internet usage. Another activity is when the government snoops on its citizens to gather information about    preventing    crime    and    terrorism..

## _How Snooping is Done_

You can do data snooping professionally and ethically (as mentioned in the examples above), misleadingly    and    unethically,    or    just misleadingly out of ignorance.

Snoopers often gain the opportunity to snoop with the help of public wi-fi networks. Most people find joy in knowing there are free wireless networks available, but they should also be aware of the risks that come with using them.

If someone gains access to your device through public wifi, they can see all the contents on the device like what the owner would, such as passwords, photos, videos, contacts, apps... name it, they can probably see it.

Not only that but they can also infiltrate your devices using your home wifi especially if there are vulnerabilities on your system that they can use for a possible entry. Still, your home is probably the least possible area that you'll be hacked, so as long as you have the proper security measures in place, then you're good.

## *Wifi Hacking "Hierarchy"*

Where would you most likely be hacked? You're most likely to be hacked, or at least your data would be snooped on, inside the office where there are lots of businesses or computers operating.

Next, there would be lower risks when you're on the road, airport, subway, café, or restaurant. Slightly lower risks come with public spaces like parking lots, parks, or other recreational areas. Then, you're safer to connect to a city-wide wifi network.

Compared to the previous ones, risks are definitely lower when you connect at home in a mixed (residential and commercial) neighborhood, or if it's in a dense neighborhood with lots of houses, or in a house over a long range with wireless ISPs around.

Lastly, the safest you could connect to is at your home, especially when it's far from the other houses, in a secluded location with a secure connection.

*How to Prevent Snooping*

How do you ensure that no one gets to see your activities or snoops into your networks?

- One, you can secure your wifi router with a complex password. Make sure to know how to access your router's GUI or control panel so that you'll always know how to change the password when necessary.
- Two, create a password that's hard to guess. Avoid using birthdays, anniversaries, or any other significant digits. Aside from creating difficult passwords, you should also change them regularly.
- Three, you should also make sure to turn off WPA encryption because that's the easiest to hack.
- Four, as much as you can, don't connect to public wifi networks. If it's a must that you should connect to one, then don't access sites such as those with banking information to prevent its exposure to those prying eyes.

Securing your wifi network is one of the best actions you could perform to prevent snooping.

Hide your information from other eyes; don't give them chances to gain access to your data.

Those are just six of the common IT security threats that you might face. Don't take these threats lightly, thinking you can always avoid them – it's just waiting for an opportunity to enter your systems and wreak havoc so you should always be prepared.

# Chapter 6 – Common Practices for Threat Mitigation

In today's world that seems to revolve and depend on technology, protecting your assets has become a paramount task, well-placed high up on the hierarchy, in fact. That's why threats have to be mitigated at the earliest possible to prevent further damage.

In this chapter, learn about the common practices for threat mitigation.

**Keep your systems updated.**

Plan for failure. Planning for failure doesn't mean you'll spend time waiting for the next security breach to infect your files, but it's actually the other way around – you should always keep yourself prepared. Doing so will minimize the consequences should an infection indeed take place.

System failures happen too often simply because patches weren't installed properly. If there are updates older than a year that aren't installed, then risks for attacks get significantly higher. On the other hand, systems that are under standard maintenance have lower attack surfaces.

Make sure everything is updated – that includes all servers for laptops, desktops, and other gadgets and mobile devices. Mobile phones should have particular operating systems or firmware with patches that can be maintained to ensure proper security. Have backup systems in place so that you can react quickly in case of threats and security issues.

**Manage passwords properly.**

In some (shocking) instances, there are companies that still set their passwords as "default" or "admin" without changing them to those more complex ones. IT professionals can change passwords later , but if they don't, then vulnerabilities can occur. Other than having weak passwords, infrequent password changes will also affect systems and lead to vulnerabilities.

Mitigate the risks of poor password management by implementing technical standards in enforcing password changes. Create alphanumeric passwords that contain both uppercase and lowercase letters, numbers, and special characters. Don't use passwords that correspond to personal information, such as your or a loved one's birthday, phone number, or any related information.

Password sharing should also not be allowed. Every employee must have their own login credentials to be used on their own systems. Plus, all stored passwords should be encrypted in compliance with specific standards.

**Make use of two-factor authentication.**

To mitigate threats, it'll also help to implement two-factor authentication. Also referred to as dual factor or two-step verification, two-factor authentication (2FA) serves as an extra security layer for your systems as it helps address the vulnerabilities of using passwords on systems.

In 2FA, two varying authentication factors are given by the user so their credentials and their resources are protected better. Aside from the usual password, users provide a second factor such as a biometric factor or a security token.

When several defenses are put in place – and in this case, the password plus 2FA – the attacker will end up trying several strategies just to get through security. It still won't guarantee your systems from being *completely* protected against attacks, but it definitely lessens the chances of your systems from being infected.

**Have a proper IT Security education.**

You could be paranoid and all – well, that's for good reason – but every day, you and your IT security team would have to come up with decisions that will either make or break your risk level.

A security awareness program would also help ensure that everyone is aware of their responsibilities toward security concerns. This is achieved through regular communication with your employees, a detailed checklist of tasks that should be accomplished by everyone, as well as a handbook that they can rely on should they get confused about anything.

The better the education you've given your team, the better the decisions and actions they will make. More so, there will be fewer chances for them to create issues for the company regarding IT security, such as plugging in a USB drive that you picked up somewhere in the company computer.

Security training, as well as instances of refresher training, can be conducted as necessary. This could be conducted once they join your team and during regular intervals. Of course, you should have training whenever incidents occur, but you shouldn't wait for these incidents before you inform your employees of what to do and what to expect.

**Be mindful of hardware security as well.**

Companies often pay close attention to cloud security, but end up neglecting hardware security. Sure, it may save your time and energy to focus and prioritize a single cloud structure for hundreds of your employees, but securing their workstations will give you a better grasp of your security systems.

Taking the necessary steps to protect your hardware would help you by not only maintaining your PCs and ensuring they're always in perfect working condition, but also by giving you that peace of mind knowing all data is in its proper place, and not accessed by unauthorized individuals.

**Take advantage of useful applications.**

You don't have to do everything on your own. If there are applications that would make your life easier, then utilize them for your systems.

Applications that would be helpful include:

- LastPass – This would allow a user to store data and even autofill information such as usernames, passwords, and even credit card information.
- YubiKey – This software is a cheap yet safe method of protecting your company

and your stored information from phishing attempts. It's not too complicated to use YubiKey, and sometimes, all you need is Gmail to implement it.

- 1Password – This stores all passwords inside a "master password" – users only need to remember one password, and everything is stored inside. No need to worry about the rest of the stored passwords – they are encrypted using the strong AES-256 algorithm.

- Duo – This app gives you an extensive range of security solutions, one of which being two-factor authentication. To verify the user's identity, you'll need two things: something you have (a token or a mobile phone, perhaps), and something you know (password). Duo is strong enough to secure your information but simple enough for everyone to easily understand.

Those are just some of the applications that you can use to protect your systems. Choose which among those fit your needs the most, so you can utilize them and further secure your information.

**Perform round-the-clock monitoring.**

You can have everything within your reach – high-end applications, educated IT staff, and updated hardware, but if you don't have someone or something monitoring your systems round the clock, then there's still a great risk of your data getting compromised.

Various services are available to remotely monitor your systems from top to bottom, making sure you're free from security threats. To add, these programs also exert efforts to avoid vulnerability through patches and security updates. Upon installation of these programs, you have set a protective shield for your system.

Other than monitoring your systems, recording the events should be a priority as well. Of course your security systems shouldn't be breached, but if they do, make sure you have documented the events. Don't worry if the data you're monitoring seem useless – the reason for a breach may not always be evident, so make sure you can track backwards.

**Is your web traffic genuine?**

For an online business, one of the major factors is the traffic it gets from genuine users. Web traffic has an essential role in generating revenue and it also helps in expanding the business. This is why not monitoring web traffic could lead to unpleasant effects for a business.

Got an online site or business? Almost half of the web traffic your website is receiving comes from non-human sources, some good and some bad. The bad bots are the ones you should be wary of because they generate bogus traffic, causing damage to your systems.

What could this bad traffic lead to?

- Google AdSense Termination – If advertising bodies would see fake views in your system or site, then they'd think of it as a form of fraud and could lead to you being penalized. Repetition of this thread may lead to your website getting blacklisted.

- Poor Sales Conversion – Bots produce bogus traffic. When the bots flood your form pages with fake details, they generate fake leads. These kinds of leads affect your sales conversion.

- Higher Bandwidth and Server Costs – In just a short time frame, your website could have millions of unwanted requests because of the bots. These requests would lead to higher and unnecessary bandwidth and server costs.

- Damaged Search Engine Capability and Website Reputation – Your page may have a million views, but if it's all fake and just produced by malicious bots, then your website won't be indexed by the search engines. Your SEO gets damaged, plus the reputation you've worked so hard for your site can just swiftly go down the drain.

That being said, it's important that you understand the source of your traffic and ensure that the traffic is from legit sources.

**Protect your systems from insider threats.**

Of course, it's a given to protect your data from outsiders, but sometimes, you fail to realize that you also have to protect them from internal threats. Outside threats are caused by hackers with wicked objectives, when on the other hand, insider threats can be caused by a careless, or worse, an employee with malicious intent.

Insider attacks can come in different forms:

- Trap Doors – Trap doors are login programs that developers come up with to have unauthorized access. Developers could add a specific code on login programs so anyone can log in using the login name, regardless of the password used. Once the code is inserted on a working program, then the login attempt will be successful.

- Login Spoofing – This is a method of collecting user passwords. In login spoofing, a login interface that mimics the real login page is mounted. The user enters their login credentials, not knowing that the page they're entering their information on is hacked, and the details they're entering will be logged into the intruder's database. The dummy shell will then be destroyed, and the user will be asked to reenter the information, this time, on the real login page.
- Logic Bombs – Logic bombs are codes embedded inside programs that are set to explode once specific conditions are satisfied. Conditions include but are not limited to a specific day or date, absence or presence of certain files, a specific person using the system, etc. Once the bomb is triggered, it can change or delete data, leading to defects on the machine.

For further protection, constant monitoring would greatly help. Heavy encryption would also contribute to protecting your systems further.

# Chapter 7 – Tools Used in the Industry

In the IT security industry, what are the tools used to make things easier and more secure?

**Antivirus Protection Programs**

A lot of people use the terms 'antivirus' and 'firewall' interchangeably, thinking they're synonymous with one another. It's really not mandatory that you have both, but having both will give you an extra layer of security.

Antivirus protection programs send alerts regarding virus and malware infections. Other programs include email scanners to ensure even the absence of web links or email attachments, and there are some that can quarantine possible threats and remove them completely.

Among the numerous antivirus programs available at the market, surely there's one that will fit you and your business needs the most.

**Firewalls**

As hackers and cybercriminals find more ways to get into systems regardless of defenses becoming stronger, you'd think that having a firewall is pointless. This shouldn't be the case – a firewall is still one of the core tools of security and is one of the most important.

Firewalls are important tools that help maintain security in your system. Often working together with antivirus programs, firewalls monitor not only network traffic but also connection attempts as it decides whether to pass freely on the computer or network.

A firewall is undoubtedly useful, but it does have its limitations. Skilled hackers found ways to create programs that fool firewalls into thinking they are reliable and that they are trustworthy. Despite the limitations, firewalls are still effective in keeping malicious attacks away.

**Penetration Tests**

Another way that you can test your systems' security systems is through penetration testing.

In a penetration test, IT professionals will try to use the same methods used by hackers to infiltrate your system. They'll check for possible vulnerabilities and weak areas. Penetration tests will simulate attacks done by hackers, such as code injection, password cracking, snooping, and even phishing.

After the penetration test is completed, the IT professionals will send you a copy of their findings; they may also give recommendations on how you could improve your security and further strengthen your defense against hackers.

## Detection Services

Detecting malicious activity is no longer limited to antivirus programs and firewalls. Hackers and cybercriminals have become advanced as well, so you have to prepare your systems with stronger forms of defense.

Installing programs that fight threats as they come (antivirus, firewalls) is good, but having something that is proactive and can see attacks before they could cause damage is better.

It's more preferable to have services that react to and identify potential security issues so that you can face and fix them as early as possible. It'll bring less damage if you're just identifying and removing attacks before they could cause any problems instead of fighting attacks that have already left footprints on your systems.

## Public Key Infrastructure (PKI)

A public key infrastructure or PKI is a group of policies needed to create, manage, and distribute digital certificates. A PKI system is necessary to identify and authenticate people, devices, and services.

Most people associate PKI only with TLS or SSL – technologies that are responsible for server associations and are the reason for the "HTTPS" and padlock icon that you see on your address bar. SSL, of course, is a given when it comes to both public sites and internal networks, but PKI also has its own place when talking about organizations' security procedures.

PKIs can perform various tasks. It can enable access control and multi-factor authentication, digitally sign and protect codes, provide encryption to email communications as well as authenticate the sender's identity, create trusted digital signatures, and build an identity to IoT ecosystems.

The aforementioned cybersecurity tools each play a role in strengthening your system's security. Some of them may require you to shell out funds, but it will prove to be profitable and cost-effective in the long run. Failing to have these in your systems will make you an easy target – recovery from damage will prove to be more expensive and take much of your precious time.

# Chapter 8 – Common Industry Tools / Terminology

It's also important that you are aware of the common tools and terminologies in this field. Being familiarized with them will also keep you updated and in-the-know about the ins and outs of IT security.

Here are some of the t ools  commonly used for IT security.

# Nagios

Nagios monitors hosts, systems, and networks, delivering alerts in real-time. Users can specify exactly what they want to be notified of. The program can monitor network services including HTTP, NNTP, ICMP, POP3, and SMTP among others. Nagios is one of the most powerful free tools for cybersecurity professionals.

# Splunk

Splunk is a fast and versatile network monitoring tool. One of the more user-friendly programs with a unified interface. Splunk's strong search function makes application monitoring easy. Splunk is a paid app with free versions available. This is an excellent tool to put on the list for those who have a budget to work with. Any information security professional with a strong enough client base should invest in Splunk.

# Burp Suite

Burp Suite is a real-time network security scanner designed to identify critical weaknesses. Burp Suite will determine how cyber security threats might invade a network, via a simulated attack. The suite is available in three versions: Community, Professional, and Enterprise. Professional and Enterprise are paid application testing tools including the web vulnerability scanner. The Community version is free but severely limited. Burp Suite is a critical application security testing tool.

# Wireshark

Use Wireshark to view traffic in as much detail as you want. Use Wireshark to follow network streams and find problems. Wireshark runs on Windows, Linux, FreeBSD or OSX based systems.

# Nessus

The Nessus Remote Security Scanner allows your IT team to scan computers remotely for security vulnerabilities. Nessus provides a detailed list of any vulnerabilities that hackers could make use of to access your computer. Nessus is free to use, although it is no longer open-source. Today, Nessus is one of the top vulnerability scanners enabling you to handle malware, common vulnerabilities and hackers in your system.

Here is some of the terminology commonly used for IT security.

## Bot / Botnet

The bot, a shortened term of the word "robot", is defined as a computer that is compromised through a malware infection. Bots can be controlled by cyber criminals – they would then use the bot to come up with more attacks. Computers infected by bots spread the same infection in their intranet, which leads to the creation of botnets.

The botnet, on the other hand, is the term used to refer to a group of compromised computers. Botnets would be handled by a command and control center giving them directions on what malicious actions would they take.

Usually, the users in the botnet are unaware that they are part of one and are responsible for malicious activities. The actions they perform include sending spam emails, ransomware, phishing scams, and DDoS attacks.

There are three types of bad bots:

- Spam bots – These bots often target blog comment sections, community portals, and lead collection forms. You'd find them in user conversations and you'd see them suddenly post unwanted links, advertisements, and banners. If people in these forums aren't too careful, they could end up clicking links that are malicious in nature such as sites that would ask them to provide sensitive personal information.

- Scraper bots – Scraper bots are filled with malicious intent, as they tend to steal content. Scrapers create bots to check out prices and product catalogs to dig deep and find out that website's pricing strategies. Competitors usually go for third-party scrapers for this act – if the targeted website ends up unprotected and vulnerable, then its competitive advantage is then known to the scrapers, and definitely to the competition.

- Scalper bots – Scalper bots, as its name implies, go for ticketing websites and make purchases in bulk. The bots purchase a huge number of tickets – sometimes even by the hundreds – and once bookings open, they then would sell the tickets at reseller websites way higher than the original cost. Because of the scalper bots, legitimate ticketing websites could end up losing clients, as they won't be able to purchase tickets at their original price.

Computers often get infected by bots through a weak security system. To fix this, virus and malware programs, as well as definitions, should have the necessary patches and updates. Computer users should also be aware of the consequences should they open unknown attachments as well as click on suspicious executables.

## Breach / Security Breach

A security breach is the unauthorized access of data on networks, devices, or servers. When hackers get to bypass security on those mentioned systems, then it leads to data leakage.

These breaches are often used within organizations, companies, or governmental institutions where the defenses were bypassed for the hackers to view and utilize confidential information such as sensitive personal details, email addresses, financial data, and other related information.

Well-known cases of security breaches include those of the following:

1. eBay (2014) – The systems of eBay were hacked; passwords of 145 million users were stolen, as well as their names, physical and email addresses, phone numbers, and dates of birth. Fortunately, credit card information wasn't included among the compromised data. Users however are warned against the possibility of phishing attacks.

2. Marriott (2018) – Marriott received an internal alert in September notifying them of an attempt to access their guest reservation database. After an investigation, it was determined that an unauthorized party has made itself a copy and even encrypted the information. In November, the information was decrypted, and they confirmed that the details were indeed the information of

500 million guests who made reservations at Starwood properties.

3. AdultFriendFinder (2016) – The dating and hookup site was hacked in 2016, exposing 412 million accounts inside it. What made it controversial was that there were .gov and .mil email addresses used to register Friend Finder Network. Even those deleted accounts that weren't purged completely were identified. Reports state how a vulnerability researcher has made its way inside its internal databases, and the hackers took advantage of it to gain access. Affected accounts were immediately informed to change their passwords to stronger ones.

4. Equifax (2017 / 2018) – A breach was first reported on 2017, stating how personal data has been exposed, including phone numbers, driver's license numbers, email addresses, Social Security numbers, and dates of birth – definitely highly valuable information. Equifax didn't give any specifics about the breach and how specifically would the owners and the accounts be affected, but offered to give credit protection services to affected individuals. Unfortunately for them, things got messed up; they sent clients to

fraudulent websites and even gave them malware downloaders.

As you can see, security breaches have to be taken seriously as their effects can be detrimental to a company. The events prove that it's never too early to protect your site and be aware of the necessary IT security measures.

## BYOD

BYOD, which stands for Bring Your Own Device, refers to employees bringing their own gadgets such as laptops, smartphones, and tablets to use inside the office and to connect on the company's secure network.

Employees are today expected to use their own devices at work, making IT security a cause of concern. Companies have set their policies with regard to BYOD, clearly setting the rules on this, so that the IT team can better manage the devices and make sure that network security won't be compromised by their own employees.

## Biometrics

Biometric security or biometrics is a method of security used to authenticate and give access to an area or system using someone's unique physical characteristics, such as the iris or retina part of the eye, voice pattern, or fingerprint patterns. These unique biological traits confirm a person's identity.

Biometrics is one of the preferred security methods for a place or system because it can be pretty difficult to break into it. The devices used for biometrics play a major role in verifying someone's identity.

Let's get to know the processes involved in biometric security.

## 1. *Iris and Retina Recognition*

Retina scanners authenticate individuals through the blood vessels at the back of their eyes. Every individual's blood vessels are unique, hence a secure method of authentication. This is considered a quite intrusive method, because it can be seen as a method that can invade your medical privacy.

Iris scanners that measure one's iris pattern are more preferable. Every person has a different iris color pattern, and this is what's being verified by the scanner. This is often used in the security field.

## 2. *Fingerprint Recognition*

Out of the three, fingerprint scanners are the least intrusive as their only concern are the fingerprints. Scanners measure the loop, whorl, and arch patterns of the fingerprint, which is unique to every individual. To add, fingerprint scanners are the cheapest and are the easiest to implement.

Fingerprint scanners are also preferred because they don't invade any privacy issues – no medical information is released, whatsoever. Because of their effectiveness and popularity, fingerprint scanners are now used even on cars and mobile devices.

### 3. *Voice Pattern Recognition*

Voice pattern recognition, or voice biometrics, works by digitizing someone's speech to produce a stored voice model or template. This software aims to identify, differentiate, and validate someone's voice. It evaluates someone's voice biometrics, e.g., natural accent, frequency, and flow of the voice.

Voice pattern recognition is different from speech recognition. Voice pattern recognition deals with the sounds made by the concerned individual, where as speech recognition, also known as voice command, allows the individual to interact with technology and control certain devices by speaking to them.

If combined, speech and voice pattern recognition can be a strong security measure, offering convenience and authentication in just one go.

## **Digital Signature**

Another security measure used often is a digital signature. A digital signature is similar to an electronic fingerprint. Through a coded message, a digital signature would securely associate a document with a signer in a recorded transaction.

Digital signatures utilize the 'public key infrastructure' or the PKI to achieve the highest levels of security and attain universal acceptance. Just like handwritten signatures, digital signatures are unique to every signer. Digital signature solution providers e.g., DocuSign follow the PKI wherein providers are required to use mathematical algorithms in generating the public and private keys.

Once the signer places his signature on the document electronically, the digital signature will be produced using the signer's private key. This key is always kept secure by the signer.

The mathematical algorithm will be the cipher, which creates data that matches the signed document, becoming the hash, and the data will then be encrypted. This encrypted data becomes the digital signature, with the indication of when the document was signed. The digital signature will be invalidated should the document be changed after signing.

To ensure the signature's integrity, as per the PKI, keys should be made, conducted, and saved in secure locations as well as utilize assistance from a Certificate Authority, i.e., a third party organization accepted as a reliable entity to ensure the security of the keys and the digital certificates.

## Encryption

Considered as one of the most essential methods in data security, encryption is defined as the method of translating data into a secret code.

In encryption, plaintext (unencrypted data) or a different form of data is converted: from readable form, it will become an encoded version that only an entity with a specific decryption key can decode.

There are two types of encryption: *symmetric* and *asymmetric encryption* .

- Asymmetric encryption, also known as public key encryption, is a form of cryptographic system with two keys: one, a public key that's known to everyone, and two, a private or secret key that's just known to specific individuals, or even just to the intended recipient of the message. What's important with this system is that both keys must be related in a way that only the messages can only be encrypted using the public key, and they can only be decrypted with the private key.

- Symmetric encryption, on the other hand, is when encryption and decryption use the same key. This is faster compared to asymmetric encryption, but it involves the sender exchanging the key used for data encryption with the receiver before the receiver can decrypt the data. The Advanced Encryption Standard (AES) is the symmetric key cipher that's most widely used.

The goal of encryption is to protect digital data and maintain its confidentiality, as well as prevent third parties from illegally accessing and modifying data. It's now a vital part of various products and services to protect data that are both stored and in transit.

## IP Address

An Internet Protocol address or an IP address is a numeric address assigned to a device that's connected to a computer network using the Internet protocol to communicate.

The IP address is quite similar to your home address. It allows people to find out where you are. With an IP address, people can detect your computer's exact location, right down to your latitude and longitude, plus, give you information about your hosting provider. Your computer can also connect to other computers through your IP address.

In essence, your IP address makes it possible for you to connect to the Internet, drown yourself in Netflix, and check out your social media accounts.

*Two Types of IP Addresses*

There are two types of IP addresses: static and dynamic IP address.

- Static IP Address – This is the type of IP address that doesn't get changed once assigned to a device on a particular network. This form is cost-effective, but could bring security risks. This is often used by email, gaming, and web servers that don't care about exposing or hiding their locations.

- Dynamic IP Address – This IP address type changes every time the device logs in to the network. Businesses and companies prefer this type because this is tougher to trace.

## Vulnerability

Vulnerability, when it comes to security, is defined as the flaw in the system that can possibly lead to an attack. It can also pertain to a form of weakness in a computer system. More often than not, it's an unintended flaw on a code or system.

Vulnerability in computer systems will not always be a risk in itself – it will only be one if those with malicious intent will use that vulnerability to exploit, and end up compromising the system.

_Common Vulnerability Threats_

Here are a few examples of common threats to guard against within your application:

# DOS Attack

A **Denial-of-Service (DoS) attack** is an attack meant to shut down a machine or network, making it inaccessible to its intended users. DoS attacks accomplish this by flooding the target with traffic, or sending it information that triggers a crash. In both instances, the DoS attack deprives legitimate users (i.e. end users, members, or account holders) of the service or resource they expected.

There are two methods of DoS attacks: flooding services or crashing services. Flood attacks occur when the system receives too much traffic for the server to buffer, causing them to slow down and eventually stop. Popular flood attacks include:

- **Buffer overflow attacks** – the most common DoS attack. The concept is to send more traffic to a network address than the programmers have built the system to handle. It includes the attacks listed below, in addition to others that are designed to exploit bugs specific to certain applications or networks
- **ICMP flood** – leverages misconfigured network devices by sending spoofed packets that ping every computer on the targeted network, instead of just one specific machine. The network is then triggered to amplify the traffic. This attack is also known as the smurf attack or ping of death.
- **SYN flood** – sends a request to connect to a server, but never completes the <u>handshake</u> . Continues until all open ports are saturated with requests and none are available for legitimate users to connect to.

Other DoS attacks simply exploit vulnerabilities that cause the target system or service to crash. In these attacks, input is sent that takes advantage of bugs in the target that subsequently crash or severely destabilize the system, so that it can't be accessed or used.

# DDOS Attack

A DDoS attack, or distributed denial-of-service attack, is similar to DoS, but is more forceful. It's harder to overcome a DDoS attack. It's launched from several computers, and the number of computers involved can range from just a couple of them to thousands or even more.

Since it's likely that not all of those machines belong to the attacker, they are compromised and added to the attacker's network by malware. These computers can be distributed around the entire globe, and that network of compromised computers is called botnet.

Since the attack comes from so many different IP addresses simultaneously, a DDoS attack is much more difficult for the victim to locate and defend against.

# SQL Injection Attack

SQL injection attacks are designed to target data-driven applications by exploiting security vulnerabilities in the application's software. They use malicious code to obtain private data, change and even destroy that data, and can go as far as to void transactions on websites.

# Man-in-the-middle Attack

Man-in-the-middle attacks are cybersecurity attacks that allow the attacker to eavesdrop on communication between two targets. It can listen to a communication which should, in normal settings, be private.

Here are just some of the types of MITM attacks:

- DNS spoofing
- HTTPS spoofing
- IP spoofing
- ARP spoofing
- SSL hijacking
- Wi-Fi hacking

*Kinds of Vulnerabilities*

What are the examples of other possible vulnerabilities on your system? Here are some of them, as well as possible ways to deal with them:

**Scenario** : You don't have the basic precautions. Your system doesn't have the latest updates, software patches, and updated virus definitions. You haven't automated the updates, and so, there are some that haven't been installed yet.

***What to do*** : Automate your updates. Whenever there are updates (especially those essential ones), download and install them immediately.

**Scenario** : You're using weak passwords. You've elected to go for default ones, such as "admin" or "password123", or you've chosen your birthday as your password.

***What to do*** : Use complex passwords. Don't use passwords that can easily be guessed. Use alphanumeric characters with uppercase and lowercase letters plus special characters.

**Scenario:** You don't have backups of your files. And if you do, you haven't tested them if they're indeed working.

***What to do*** : Create backup files of your data, and don't forget to check them if your backup is working. One of the biggest mistakes you could make is to have backups but not test them.

**Scenario:** You don't deal with possible insider security threats. Sure, you've secured your servers and updated everything as needed, but have you dealt with the employees that are departing, especially those that are bored and disgruntled?

***What to do:*** Every user should have specified limited access to the system. Ensure everyone knows how to change their passwords. Once an employee resigns, you should immediately suspend and delete their user accounts and prevent them from gaining access to your system.

**Scenario:** You haven't trained your employees about social engineering. They haven't been informed of the risks that come with social engineering, and so, wouldn't be ready should they face such.

***What to do*** : Hackers use social engineering to trick people and have them divulge private and secure information. Educate your employees about this so that they don't fall prey into this kind of security breach.

Other ways to address vulnerabilities are the following:

- Use tools that scan vulnerability. There are tools that scan unpatched software, open ports, and other weaknesses. Some scan the network, some scan the device, and some scan both.
- Understand those other common attacks that can target your network. There are times when attackers don't have a specific target and just go for those with open systems .

As you can see, it's up to the hackers to use the vulnerabilities for their own good. Don't give them the opportunity to do so – eliminate the vulnerabilities and keep your systems safe from hackers. Employ some best practices for IT Security and shore up any vulnerabilities that could lead to your organization becoming a victim of a serious breach.

# Conclusion

I'd like to thank you and congratulate you for transiting my lines from start to finish.

I hope this book was able to help you to understand the concepts surrounding IT security, and you have at least realized the importance of having IT security measures implemented in your organization or computer systems.

The next step is to inspect your systems and determine – "Do I have enough protection for my systems? Are there vulnerable areas that hackers can penetrate and get through? Is there something else I need to do?"

Use this book as a basic guide on how you could protect yourself when it comes to IT Security. Soon, you'll take pride in having a secure network, and give yourself peace of mind knowing your data is safe from prying eyes.

I wish you the best!

Visit www.rmstechnologyconsulting.com for more titles in this series.

Visit www.itjobhacks.com for the best real world, hands on IT tutorials and courses.

## Other titles you might like:

Stress Free Cloud Migration

"A Practical Guide To The Cloud"

STRESS FREE

Cloud Migration

Best Practices For A Successful
Migration Of Applications
To The Cloud

Volume 1- Planning The Migration

RMS Technology Consulting

Surviving Agile For QA Professionals

Surviving

# AGILE

For
QA Professionals

Best Practices For Testing In A Rapid Development Cycle

RMS Technology Consulting